What if we do
NOTHING?

POVERTY

Cath Senker

**Consultant: Rob Bowden, Specialist in
Global Environmental and Social Issues**

WORLD ALMANAC® LIBRARY

Please visit our web site at: www.garethstevens.com
For a free color catalog describing World Almanac® Library's list of
high-quality books and multimedia programs, call 1-800-848-2928 (USA)
or 1-800-387-3178 (Canada). World Almanac® Library's fax: (414) 332-3567.

Library of Congress Cataloging-in-Publication Data

Senker, Cath.
    Poverty / Cath Senker.
      p. cm. – (What if we do nothing?)
    Includes bibliographical references and index.
    ISBN-13: 978-0-8368-7757-1 (lib. bdg.)
    ISBN-13: 978-0-8368-8157-8 (softcover)
    1. Poverty–Juvenile literature. 2. Poor–Health and hygiene–Juvenile
literature. 3. Poor–Education–Juvenile literature. 4. Poverty–Prevention–
Juvenile literature. I. Title.
    HC79.P6.S45   2007
    339.4'6–dc22   2006030447

First published in 2007 by
World Almanac® Library
A Member of the WRC Media Family of Companies
330 West Olive Street, Suite 100
Milwaukee, WI 53212 USA

Copyright © 2007 by World Almanac® Library.

Produced by Arcturus Publishing Limited
Editor: Nicola Barber
Designer: Peta Phipps
Consultant: Rob Bowden

World Almanac® Library editorial direction: Valerie J. Weber
World Almanac® Library editor: Leifa Butrick
World Almanac® Library art direction: Tammy West
World Almanac® Library graphic design: Charlie Dahl
World Almanac® Library production: Jessica Yanke and Robert Kraus

Picture credits: CORBIS: cover background (Thomas Mukoya/Reuters), cover top
inset (Andrew Holbrooke), 6 (Issei Kato/Reuters), 9 (Thomas Mukoya/Reuters), 11
(Alexander Natruskin/Reuters), 16 (Robert Essel NYC), 21 (Reuters), 22 (Rickey
Rogers/Reuters), 30 (Janet Jarman), 32 (Guillaume Bonn), 35 (Beawiharta/
Reuters), 36 (Amit Bhargava), 41 (Reuters), 43 (Jose Miguel Gomez/Reuters),
44 (Rafiqur Rahman/Reuters). EASI-Images: 12 (Rob Bowden), 18 (Rob Bowden),
24 (Chris Fairclough), 27 (Rob Bowden), 30 (Roy Maconachie). Rex Features: cover
bottom inset (Patrick Clarke), 5 (Tony Waltham/Robert Harding), 14 (Andrew
Aiken), 29 (Patrick Clarke).

The author would like to acknowledge the following sources of quoted material:
Jeremy Seabrook *The No-Nonsense Guide to World Poverty*: 8 (Tanzanian woman),
11 (Farida Bibi); Jubilee Zambia: 16 (Besinati Mpopo); Naomi Klein *No Logo*: 29;
NBC website (reporter Charlene Gubash): 36 (Zoya). The material on pages 4 (Munni),
5 (UK poverty), 14 (Monique), 26 (Maryama) is adapted by the publisher from
www.oxfam.org.uk (2006) with the permission of Oxfam GB, Oxfam House, John
Smith Drive, Cowley, Oxford OX4 2JY UK. Oxfam GB does not necessarily endorse any
text or activities that accompany the materials, nor has it approved the adapted text.

Printed in China

1 2 3 4 5 6 7 8 9 10 09 08 07 06

Contents

CHAPTER 1

Patterns of Poverty

It is 2015. Eighteen-year-old Munni from Mirzapur in Uttar Pradesh, India, is training to be a teacher. Munni comes from a *dalit* family, the lowest class in Indian society. About 50 percent of the dalits live below the poverty line. Few have had a chance to get an education; most have no electricity in their homes. Munni and her family have no land and are forced to move from place to place so that her parents can find agricultural work. When she was nine, Munni started to attend a school set up by a local nonprofit aid organization. She was the first in her family to receive an education. Munni's income as a teacher will help her family, but she and her family still have no land, no permanent home, and little access to health or other social services. It will be hard for this young woman to break out of poverty.

Nearly half the people who live in poverty live in South Asia. The aim of the Millennium Development Goals (MDGs) adopted by the United Nations (UN) in 1990 was to halve the proportion of people living in absolute poverty by 2015. Although poverty has been reduced in many countries, 380 million people still are extremely poor.

THE UN MILLENNIUM DEVELOPMENT GOALS

By 2015, all UN member states have pledged to meet these goals:

1. Eradicate extreme poverty and hunger
2. Achieve universal primary education
3. Promote gender equality and empower women
4. Reduce child mortality
5. Improve maternal health
6. Combat HIV/AIDS, malaria, and other diseases
7. Ensure environmental sustainability
8. Create a global partnership for development

Defining Poverty

Before discussing what can be done about poverty, it is important to define it. One measure is absolute poverty. According to the UN, about 1.2 billion people live in absolute poverty, defined as an income of less than $1 a day. Many lack even basic food, clothing, and shelter. The vast majority of these people live in the developing countries of Africa, Asia, and Latin America.

Another measure is relative poverty. For example, you may live in a developed country, have a roof over your head, and go to school. If your home is cramped, however, and you can afford only the cheapest food and secondhand clothes, you are probably worse off than most others in society. Groups of people in developed countries who live in relative poverty may include the unemployed, people in temporary and low-paid work, and, often, elderly people. In many developed countries, the poorest in society live in neglected inner-city areas with run-down housing, poor schools, and inadequate transportation and recreational facilities. Life is a struggle. As an unemployed person in Great Britain explains: "Living in poverty is hard work. I spend hours running from shop to shop to get the cheapest deals at the best times of day. My days are consumed by trying to make ends meet."

Additional ways to assess poverty are linked to people's well-being. These measures include enjoying good health, not dying young, being happy and respected, and feeling part of society.

GLOBAL INCOME DISTRIBUTION

- The richest 20 percent of the world's population share 75 percent of world income.
- The poorest 40 percent of the world's people share only 5 percent of world income.
- The poorest 20 percent share just 1.5 percent of world income.

Source: Human Development Report 2005

This settlement of huts alongside the river in Coonoor in Tamil Nadu, India, is home to dalit families.

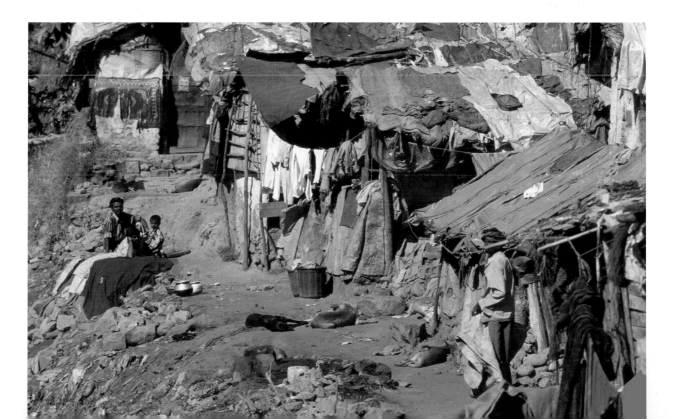

A Chinese girl in Chungqing, southwest China, performs acrobatics while she and her mother beg for money. The city is being developed as part of the Chinese government's China Western Development Strategy, but not all of its people have benefited as yet.

The Causes of Poverty

Poverty exists within all nations because people do not benefit equally from their country's economic growth. Huge inequalities also exist among nations. The roots of this wealth gap lie in history. During the period between the sixteenth and twentieth centuries, most of the present-day nations of South and Central America, Asia, and Africa were ruled by European countries as colonies. The European countries exploited their colonies for raw materials that they imported to feed their developing industries. At the same time, they prevented the colonies from developing their own industries. During the mid-twentieth century, most of the colonies gained freedom from foreign rule. It was hard, however, for these newly independent nations to compete economically with the long-established, industrialized

DEFINITIONS

Developed countries (developed market economies):
All the countries of Europe and North America plus Australia, New Zealand, and Japan

Undeveloped countries:
All the countries of Africa, Asia (excluding Japan), Latin America, and the Caribbean plus Melanesia, Micronesia, and Polynesia

6

countries. Wars, corruption, and environmental problems in some of these new nations have made existing problems worse, causing deaths, food shortages, and refugee crises that have left ever-increasing numbers of people in poverty.

Inequality and Globalization

During the twentieth century, the gap between the income of the richest and the poorest countries grew substantially. In 1990, for example, the average U.S. citizen was thirty-eight times richer than the average Tanzanian. In 2006, the average U.S. citizen was sixty-one times richer. Since the early 1980s, a process called globalization has made countries around the world increasingly interdependent and increasingly interconnected through the rapid growth of trade, communications, travel, and culture. Some developing countries, such as India and China, have benefited from globalization. The Chinese economy grew at an astounding average rate of 10 percent per year during the 1980s and 1990s. Between 1990 and 1998, the number of Chinese living on less than $1 a day fell by 150 million.

However, inequality within China also grew because the richer groups in society benefited most from rising living standards. Inequality of income has also increased in Africa, Latin America, the Caribbean, and in the countries of the former Soviet Union as well as Britain and the United States.

What If We Do Nothing?

The conventional view is that the benefits of economic growth eventually trickle down to the whole of society and end poverty. this view may not be true. After all, the world's wealth has increased enormously, but large numbers of people still live in poverty. If we do nothing to improve health, education, the environment, the use of resources, trade rules, debt relief, and aid for developing countries, then widespread poverty will continue. How can changes in these areas help alleviate poverty?

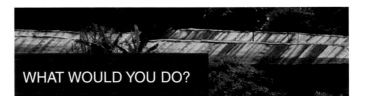

WHAT WOULD YOU DO?

You Are in Charge
Imagine that you are the prime minister of Great Britain. Once Zambia was a British colony. Today, 70 percent of the Zambian people live in poverty, and thousands die of AIDS. Which one of the United Nations millennium development goals would you like to encourage in Zambia, and what might you do to help? See page 47 for some suggestions.

CHAPTER 2

Poverty and Health

At a crisis meeting in South Africa in 2015, representatives of nonprofit aid organizations and HIV/AIDS campaigners from several sub-Saharan African countries are in despair. The statistics show that in the past year, HIV has infected another 45 million people. In 2005, the leaders of the G8, the major industrial nations, had promised to provide HIV/AIDS treatment to all who needed it by 2010, but they did not fulfill their promise. Treatments are still too costly for the poorest governments to make them freely available to their people.

As a Tanzanian woman in her sixties says, "You are poor when you have seen your seven children die of AIDS. When the people you expect to take care of you in old age die before you, who will you turn to?" In 2006, about 40 million people were living with HIV/AIDS, 95 percent of them in developing countries. In developed countries, many people with the illness have access to antiretroviral therapy, drugs that help to prolong their lives. In developing countries, most people with AIDS cannot afford the antiretroviral therapy, so a diagnosis of HIV/AIDS amounts to a death sentence. AIDS kills mostly young adults of working age, so it has a devastating effect on a country's economy and society. Children who lose their parents often have to be looked after by relatives who may already be struggling to care for their own families. Although HIV/AIDS is not a disease that is confined to the poor, it adds to the general health problems suffered by people living in poverty.

LIFE EXPECTANCY AT BIRTH IN 1970–1975 AND 2000–2005

These figures for five sub-Saharan African countries show that the HIV/AIDS crisis has caused life expectancy to drop dramatically.

Country	Life expectancy	
	1970-75	2000-05
Zambia	49.7	32.4
Zimbabwe	56	33.1
Swaziland	47.3	34.4
Central African Republic	43	39.5
Lesotho	56	35.1

Source: UN Human Development Report 2004

How Poverty Creates Illness

Other illnesses also affect the poor, including diseases spread through water. Many of the world's poorest people live in urban slums or deprived rural areas. In 2002, more than half of the world's population had access to a clean water supply through a household connection or a yard tap. However, 1.1 billion people still lacked direct access to clean water. Some used water contaminated with feces, and others became ill because their water was contaminated during transportation or storage. In Kibera, an urban slum on the outskirts of the Kenyan capital, Nairobi, people do not have running water in their homes. They share some communal water pumps, but many people are forced to buy water at high prices from water sellers. They have no sanitation facilities. Sewage runs through the alleys between the shacks. With no garbage collection or proper roads, mud and filth pile up everywhere. The dirty conditions enable disease to spread easily.

A polluted stream runs through Kibera, an urban slum in Kenya. Private dealers provide Kibera's water. These dealers lay their own pipes and charge people double the price they would pay for water outside the slum.

Children in poverty suffer from many ordinary illnesses including measles, mumps, and diarrhea. Diseases such as measles and mumps can be prevented by vaccination programs, while cheap and simple measures, such as education in cleanliness and promoting hand washing, can lead to a dramatic reduction in cases of diarrhea. Many poor people lack access to such programs and education, and if they do not have access to clean water, it is hard to maintain good standards of hygiene. Every year 1.8 million people die from diarrhea and other water-borne diseases such as cholera. Most of them— 90 percent—are children under the age of five living in developing countries. According to the World Health Organization (WHO), unsafe water supplies and inadequate sanitation and hygiene caused 88 percent of the diseases linked to diarrhea. Malaria is responsible for 1.3 million deaths and is particularly prevalent in sub-Saharan

TRACHOMA

- Trachoma is an eye disease that causes blindness if left untreated. About 84 million people in the world suffer from it, and about 8 million have been left visually impaired (unable to see properly).
- The disease is most common in the poorest and most remote rural areas of Africa, Asia, Central and South America, Australia, and the Middle East.
- An infectious disease, trachoma spreads easily in places with a shortage of clean drinking water and a lack of sanitation. It overwhelmingly strikes children and the women who care for them.
- Repeated infections cause scarring on the inside of the eyelid that can, however, be treated by simple surgery.
- The number of people affected has fallen from 360 million in 1985 through a program led by the World Health Organization that involves surgery, antibiotics to treat the infection, and improved access to clean water. The aim of the program is to eliminate trachoma by 2020.

Source: World Health Organization

Africa. Disease prevention methods and treatment could save nearly all of these lives.

Russia

What happened in Russia illustrates the links between poverty and health. After the fall of the Soviet Union in 1991, industrial production in Russia collapsed. Many people lost their jobs, and as living standards declined, alcohol abuse and drug addiction rose dramatically. Health care, badly needed to help cope with these growing problems, was no longer freely available. Between 1990 and 1994, the annual number of deaths skyrocketed by 39 percent. The incidence of tuberculosis (TB), an infectious lung disease associated with poverty, doubled during the 1990s; in 2005, Russia had one of the highest incidence rates of TB in the world.

Hunger and Malnutrition

From 2000 to 2002, 17 percent of the people in developing countries were undernourished and did not get the minimum amount of food to provide their caloric requirements. People usually go hungry because they are unable to produce enough food for their needs or earn enough money to buy it. Hunger has severe effects on health. Children who go hungry do not grow properly. In 2003, 28 percent of the children under age five in developing countries were underweight. Farida Bibi, a landless laborer from the Bay of Bengal in Bangladesh, describes hunger: "You dream of food all the time. You fear the mornings because you will wake up hungry and hear the children crying. I have picked up sugarcane that other people have eaten and thrown away, just to give the children something to chew."

This homeless Russian woman has just received a plate of food from a distribution point at a Moscow train station. Homelessness, as well as the number of homeless children, has increased in Russia since the mid-1990s.

In developed countries, many people do not necessarily go hungry but they are still technically malnourished because they do not eat a diet that provides the broad range of vitamins and minerals that are important for good health. The poorest people often cannot afford to eat a nutritious and well-balanced diet because healthy foods, such as fruits and vegetables, tend to be relatively expensive. In the United States, poor diet and lack of exercise cause high levels of obesity. Obesity is more widespread, however, among the poor. Women with low incomes in the United States are 50 percent more likely to be obese than those with higher incomes. Malnourishment also increases the risk of disease. Obese people have a high risk of developing heart disease, while in developed countries an unhealthy diet is linked to approximately one-quarter of cancer deaths.

Some Solutions

Much could be done to improve world health. If people have access to clean water, sanitation, and garbage collection facilities, they are less likely to become ill, and diseases will not be able to spread easily. Treating household water and storing it safely can lead to great improvements in water quality and reduce the number of people suffering from diarrhea and waterborne diseases. Effective ways of making household water safe include boiling it, treating it with a chemical called chlorine, or filtering it. Once treated, the water needs to be stored in a container with a narrow opening and a dispensing device, such as a faucet. Numerous surveys have indicated that simple precautions like these reduce the incidence of diarrhea by between 6 and 90 percent, depending on local conditions. A study in a refugee camp in Malawi in 2005 showed that improvements in treating and storing water resulted in a 31 percent reduction in cases of diarrhea in children under five.

Education and training are also related to disease prevention and successful treatment. International nonprofit aid organizations

This poster advises people in African countries to save water by using a leaky tin to wash their hands and faces. The tin is usually a plastic-lined can or plastic container hung from a tree branch. A small hole punched in the container allows water to drip out. Each person can wash his or her face or hands without sharing water—and possible infection—with other people.

provide many programs to educate people about safe sex methods to prevent the spread of HIV/AIDS. In Uganda, where AIDS is the second most frequently reported cause of death, health and community workers supervise patients taking their antiretroviral therapy. The workers check that patients are taking their medicine every day; they offer health advice and send patients to the hospital if they have problems. By September 2005, 67 thousand out of the estimated 114 thousand people who require treatment for HIV/AIDS in Uganda were receiving it. Uganda has one of the highest proportions of people receiving AIDS treatment in Africa.

In developed countries, as in developing countries, improving access to health services for people in poverty is fundamental. For example, in Australia, indigenous Aborigines die, on the average, seventeen years sooner than nonindigenous Australians because the indigenous community does not receive the same primary health care as non-indigenous Australians. A 2004 report estimated that it would cost up to $430 million to provide universal primary health care to Aboriginal communities. In 2006, Tom Calma, an Aboriginal Social Justice Commissioner, proposed the goal of achieving equal access to primary health care for Aboriginal people within ten years.

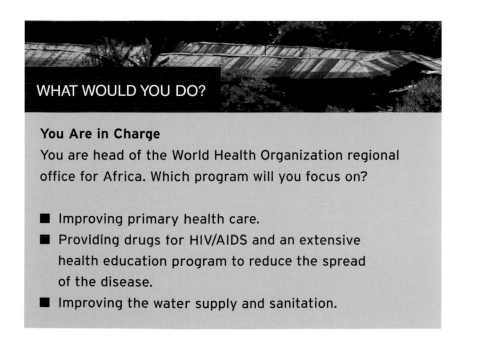

WHAT WOULD YOU DO?

You Are in Charge
You are head of the World Health Organization regional office for Africa. Which program will you focus on?

■ Improving primary health care.
■ Providing drugs for HIV/AIDS and an extensive health education program to reduce the spread of the disease.
■ Improving the water supply and sanitation.

Getting an Education

It is 2015, and Monique is fifteen years old. Like most girls in Burkina Faso, she has never been to school. The whole family made sacrifices for her brother Ekuzuna to attend primary school, but the family could not afford to send Monique or her sisters because they needed to have the girls work on the corn crop. As well as paying Ekuzuna's fees for attending school, his parents pay for paper, pens, and pencils. If she could learn to read and write, Monique could earn money to help her family, but she will probably be married off to an older cousin within a year.

In many African countries, more than half the children now complete primary school. Most countries, however, have been unable to meet the UN target of ensuring that all boys and girls complete a full course of primary schooling.

Going to School

Between 1996 and 2003 in Burkina Faso, 32 percent of the boys and 22 percent of the girls went to school, but only 81 percent of them actually completed their primary education. As is the case in many of the world's poorest countries, Burkina Faso does not have enough schools, particularly in rural areas. Legally, in Burkina Faso, classes are restricted to sixty-five children—a large number for any teacher to cope with. In many rural areas, however, classes are even bigger. Each classroom has only basic equipment—desks and a blackboard—and few teaching materials. Even though the Burkina Faso government allocates 25 percent of its budget to education, it still lacks the funds to provide education for all.

Children of different ages share a classroom in the Serengeti region of Tanzania. School fees are a major barrier that prevent children—particularly girls—from attending school. When school fees were abolished in Tanzania, Uganda, and Kenya, 7 million additional children started school in these three countries.

Advances in education are notable. The number of adults in developing countries who can read increased from 67 to 77 percent between 1990 and 2003. In 2005, however, more than 115 million primary-school-aged children still did not attend school in developing countries, and girls consistently lagged behind boys. During 2001–2002, for every one hundred boys who went to school in developing countries, an average of ninety-two girls also attended. The gender gap is wider in countries in southern Asia, sub-Saharan Africa, and Western Asia, which have few schools and resources. Families often have to choose whether to send a son or a daughter to school, and girls usually lose out because girls are not considered equal to boys. Boys are seen as more important because boys will head the family and be the main income earners when they grow up.

This map shows the low-income countries of the world as defined by the World Bank in 2005. In these countries, Gross National Income (GNI) is $875 or less per person per year. In many of these countries, education suffers due to lack of resources.

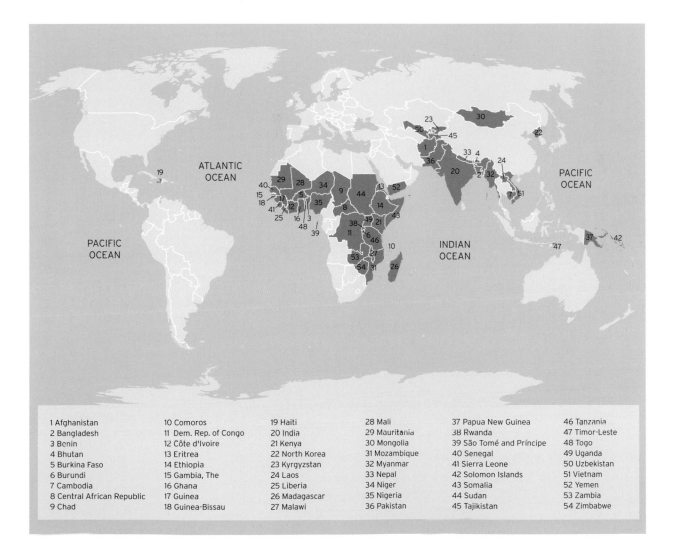

1 Afghanistan	10 Comoros	19 Haiti	28 Mali	37 Papua New Guinea	46 Tanzania
2 Bangladesh	11 Dem. Rep. of Congo	20 India	29 Mauritania	38 Rwanda	47 Timor-Leste
3 Benin	12 Côte d'Ivoire	21 Kenya	30 Mongolia	39 São Tomé and Príncipe	48 Togo
4 Bhutan	13 Eritrea	22 North Korea	31 Mozambique	40 Senegal	49 Uganda
5 Burkina Faso	14 Ethiopia	23 Kyrgyzstan	32 Myanmar	41 Sierra Leone	50 Uzbekistan
6 Burundi	15 Gambia, The	24 Laos	33 Nepal	42 Solomon Islands	51 Vietnam
7 Cambodia	16 Ghana	25 Liberia	34 Niger	43 Somalia	52 Yemen
8 Central African Republic	17 Guinea	26 Madagascar	35 Nigeria	44 Sudan	53 Zambia
9 Chad	18 Guinea-Bissau	27 Malawi	36 Pakistan	45 Tajikistan	54 Zimbabwe

Delays to Progress

For poor people, seeking an education is the obvious way to improve their job opportunities so they can rise out of poverty. In many poor countries, however, governments have cut spending on health and education to pay back their debts such as loans from wealthier countries. In some places, educational opportunities are worse than they used to be. In Zambia in 1985, nearly 100 percent of the primary-school-aged children went to school, but because the economic situation has deteriorated since then, fewer children attend school now, and the quality of the schooling has declined.

The HIV/AIDS epidemic has also had a devastating effect on the Zambian people's efforts to improve their lives through education. Two-thirds of the trained teachers have died of AIDS. Zambian mother Besinati Mpopo enjoyed high-quality schooling in the late 1970s and 1980s, but she worries about the prospects for her son Gershom if education does not improve. She asks: "Will Gershom be able to have the quality of education that I had?"

Australian Aboriginal boys use a laptop computer. Generally, the health, education, employment, and housing of indigenous Australians is not as good as that of nonindigenous Australians. Getting a better education could help raise their living standards.

The lack of schools, trained teachers, and resources present major problems. Other issues also create difficulties. In poor countries, parents often cannot afford the cost of tuition, uniforms, and books. More important, children frequently have to help with farm work or the family business. They may attend school for only a short time or not go at all. The problem has become worse because the price that farmers receive for farm goods has fallen. More work is required to make enough money from farming; like their parents, children have to work harder.

Poverty and Education

Without a good education, it is almost impossible for people to get a reasonably paid job and break out of the cycle of poverty. Poorer people, however, tend to receive less education. In Australia, for example, indigenous Aborigines generally have a lower standard of living than nonindigenous people. Although the situation is improving, in 2004 indigenous students were only half as likely as nonindigenous students to graduate from school. There are various reasons. Although schooling is free, going to school is costly because parents have to buy uniforms, books, and sports equipment. Poorer schools often have larger classes, fewer resources, and less qualified teachers. Indigenous children have health problems, especially hearing difficulties and poor nutrition. These factors make it hard for students to succeed and improve their lives.

Brain Drain

Another issue affecting education and economic development in developing countries is known as the *brain drain*. Although the developing countries of Asia and Africa educate and train doctors, nurses, and teachers, many of these workers get jobs in the developed countries of Europe and the United States when they have their degrees. Many developed countries actively recruit such workers because of shortages in their own countries. Well-trained and educated people from developing countries can usually earn far more money in developed countries than they can at home.

This pie chart shows the geographical distribution of children out of school. In 2001, nearly eight out of ten children who did not go to school lived in sub-Saharan Africa or southern Asia.

Source: UNICEF/UNESCO

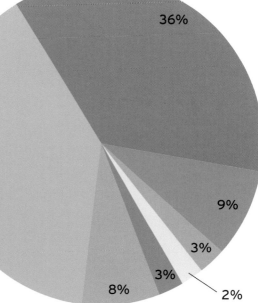

KEY

- Sub-Saharan Africa
- Southern Asia
- East Asia and Pacific countries
- Middle East and North Africa
- Central and Eastern Europe/Commonwealth of Independent States
- Latin America and Caribbean
- Industrialized countries

A 2004 report by the International Monetary Fund, for example, estimated that 60 percent of Jamaicans with a degree have migrated to the United States. The *Jamaica Gleaner*, a Jamaican newspaper, reported in 2004 that the country loses 8 percent of its registered nurses and more than 20 percent of its clinical nurse specialists each year, mostly to the United States or Great Britain. Jamaicans working abroad usually send money to Jamaica to help their families at home. The money is good for the local economy, but Jamaica's health sector is always short of staff.

Bright Ideas

New ideas can improve the educational system. Charities have come up with programs to provide education to working children that fit around their jobs and housework, such as the dalit school in Uttar Pradesh. Programs reducing school tuition, improving school buildings and the quality of teaching, and providing school lunches have encouraged families to send their children to school.

Children attend a school on a tea plantation in Kerala, India. According to the Kerala government, girls now have equal opportunity to get an education; girls represent 49 percent of all school students.

A government can make important improvements in the education system when it wants to. For example, Kerala in southern India is economically one of the poorest states in the country, yet it provides the highest levels of health care and education in the country. In 2001, the literacy rate, or number of people who can read, was 91 percent, compared to 60 percent in India overall. Schools in Kerala, unlike those in other states in India, do not have problems with the basic necessities. They have toilets, a water supply, and electricity. First through fourth grade classrooms have one teacher for every thirty students, and fifth through seventh grades have one teacher for every twenty-nine students. Only 1.5 percent of the children drop out of school in Kerala. This example shows that poverty and poor education do not necessarily go hand in hand.

Equal Access

In developed countries, the main problem is offering equal access to education for all communities. For example, migrants and refugees often find it hard to get a good job if they do not speak the language of their new country well. Sweden offers newly arrived adult migrants free, government-funded lessons in Swedish and in the country's culture. Of the developed countries, Sweden has the lowest percentage of adults lacking literacy skills and the lowest levels of poverty.

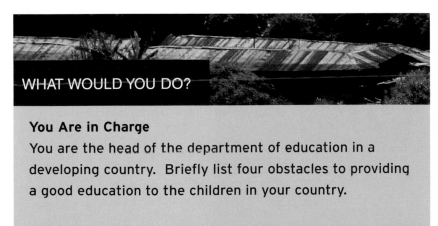

WHAT WOULD YOU DO?

You Are in Charge
You are the head of the department of education in a developing country. Briefly list four obstacles to providing a good education to the children in your country.

Which one of these might be the easiest to change? What would you do?

CHAPTER 4

Environment and Resources

Last year in 2014, Isabella's family was forced to leave their jobs at Finca Dos Marias, a coffee plantation, and abandon their home in the highlands of Guatemala. The family had grown coffee in the area for generations. In the 2000s, however, record low coffee prices led to the complete collapse of the Guatemalan coffee industry. Some families set up a cooperative, but the business failed because prices were so low that the families lost money when they sold their coffee. Isabella and her family reluctantly moved to Guatemala City where Isabella's father suffered severe depression and turned to alcohol to relieve his misery. He died recently. Now the family's only income comes from scavenging through garbage dumps and selling any goods of value that they can find.

Cash Crops

Between the middle and the end of the twentieth century, global food output nearly tripled. So why is there still hunger on a huge scale? Over the last half-century, the ever-increasing demands of the developed countries for agricultural products have led many farmers in Africa, Asia, and South and Central America to shift from traditional methods of farming to growing cash crops for sale to large transnational companies. In Guatemala, for example, many farmers grow coffee; in Ecuador, bananas are the main crop. Relying on one crop, however, can be dangerous because the prices that farmers receive often go up and down wildly, so growers are never quite sure how much they are likely to earn. Furthermore, in the long-term, prices of cash crops tend to fall because transnational companies usually seek the cheapest suppliers and will give their business to anyone who offers lower prices. In the early 2000s, for example, Vietnam became a major coffee exporter, producing coffee that was cheaper than Central and South American coffee, although of lower quality. The large quantity of cheap coffee on the world market forced the price of coffee downward and contributed to a global

This farmer from Guatemala gathers high-quality coffee beans. When the international price of coffee falls, it is hard for small-scale farmers to grow more coffee to earn more money.

collapse in coffee prices. Thousands of coffee farmers in Central and South America lost their jobs.

Environmental Problems

The enormous expansion of agricultural production has hurt the environment as well as the farmers. It has increased the exploitation of the world's forests, farmlands, seas, rivers, and energy resources. A soaring demand for meat, for example, over the past half-century, mostly in developed countries, has meant that livestock farming has increased 38 percent worldwide since 1961. To produce meat, animals eat crops and drink water. It takes the equivalent of 15.4 pounds (7 kg) of grain to produce 2.2 pounds (1 kg) of beef or lamb. Livestock farming is a far less efficient way of producing food than growing many kinds of vegetables and grains. In many places, large areas of forest are being destroyed simply to provide grazing land for cattle, goats, and pigs, or land is cleared to grow crops for animal feed.

WORLD MEAT PRODUCTION

This graph shows world meat production in kilograms per person from 1950 to 2002. World meat production rose from 48.5 million tons (44 million tonnes) to more than 264.5 million tons (240 million tonnes).

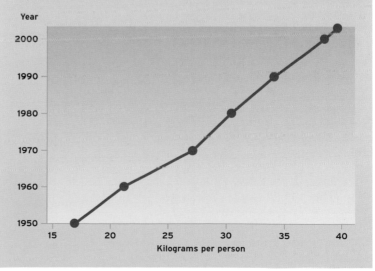

Source: UN FAO, 2003

Poverty can lead to destroying environments when people exploit them to survive. In Brazil, many landless farmers use land cleared from the rain forest to grow enough food to live on. They cut down shrubs and trees, and they burn the rest of the plants. The farmers then plant crops such as bananas, corn, or rice. After a year or two, however, the soil is no longer productive, so the farmers move on to clear another section of forest. This traditional method of farming is known as shifting cultivation. It has been carried out in a sustainable way for centuries, and the small plots, cleared and then abandoned by farmers, were allowed to regenerate. The number of people who now clear forest for cropland, however, has increased so dramatically that such clearance poses a major threat to the rain-forest environment.

Problems such as forest destruction arise because many of the world's poorest people have little, if any, choice over how to make a living. They cannot afford good land. They are often forced by their circumstances to live and work in places that richer people avoid.

Brazilian farm workers burn down felled trees to clear the land for agriculture. Trees are not the only living things that are destroyed; because of deforestation, many species of animals and plants also lose their habitat.

Poor farmers might settle in areas that are prone to flooding or landslides or where the land makes it difficult to earn a living because of problems such as unpredictable or low rainfall.

The Population Explosion

Some people argue that the rapidly growing populations of developing countries are exhausting the world's resources and creating further poverty. The United Nations predicts that the population of the world will increase from 6.5 billion in 2005 to 9 billion by 2050. Most of the increase will be in the developing countries.

Some experts argue that reducing population growth is vital for tackling poverty. In India and Bangladesh, for example, when a farm passes down to the next generation, the children divide the land. The farms become smaller and smaller and cannot support the people who live on them. Other experts claim that security is the main issue. Poor parents in developing countries rely on their children to do some of the work and to care for them when they are old. They have big families because many children die young. When parents know their children will survive, they may limit their families. People are not poor because they have too many children; rather, people have lots of children because they are poor. If a family rises out of poverty by getting some education, women will have the choice of bearing fewer children, which will reduce the population pressure on the environment.

Use of Resources

It is important to note that developing countries use fewer resources than developed countries. For example, people in the more developed world use five times more energy per person than people in the less developed world. The 5 percent of the world's population that lives in the United States consumes 23 percent of the world's energy. As countries such as China and India develop, these countries also use more resources.

Between May 2000 and August 2005, Brazil lost more than 51,000 square miles (132,000 sq km) of rain forest, an area larger than Greece. This pie chart shows the causes of this destruction.
Source: mongabay.com

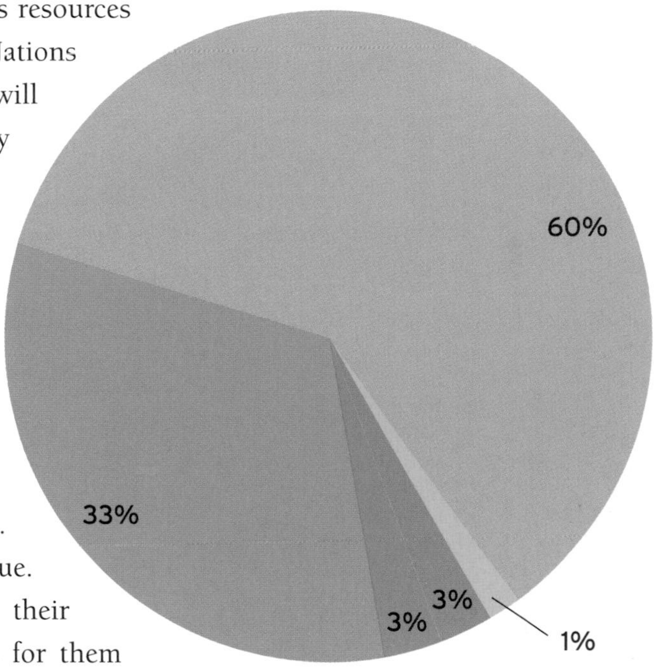

60%

33%

3%

3%

1%

KEY

- Establishing cattle ranches
- Small scale, subsistence agriculture
- Logging, legal and illegal
- Fires, mining, city growth, road construction, and dams
- Large scale, commercial agriculture

People in developing countries are often good at conserving resources. They cannot always afford to buy new things, so they reuse and recycle all kinds of items. In Kenya, for example, people make a solid fuel product called a briquette from organic waste. They collect and compress combustible materials (materials that will burn) to form the briquettes, which they burn like wood. Many of these briquettes are made from sugar bagasse—the waste fiber that is left after sugarcane is processed—and from sawdust, a waste material

Here in Nairobi, Kenya, workers make briquettes for fuel from recycled newspaper and charcoal dust collected by local people. About 80 percent of Kenyans depend on wood for their fuel, which contributes to deforestation. The use of briquettes helps to reduce dependence on wood-based fuels.

from wood processing. They also use waste paper and leaves. This reuse of waste materials conserves resources and provides employment for the people who make the briquettes as well as a cheap fuel source for poor people.

Other new ideas in developing countries help save water. In the Maikaal region of central India, local farmers invented Pepsee in the late 1990s to improve their use of water. Pepsee is a type of drip irrigation that involves applying water directly to the roots of the plants. The farmers use plastic tubing, which they buy cheaply from candy manufacturers who use it to make popsicles. The farmers place the plastic tube at the roots of the plants. If this technology were used on a large scale, it could do a lot to conserve water resources, improve crop production, and reduce poverty.

Food Solutions

One way to conserve resources is to find more efficient methods of raising animals for food or to shift to breeding animals such as poultry or farmed fish that require fewer resources than cattle. Another solution is to make cropland more productive. Small-scale, low-tech farming techniques that are suited to a specific local environment can vastly improve poor people's lives. For example, in 1996, a project began in Tigray, Ethiopia, to help farmers improve the productivity of their land by using composting techniques. The farmers treated some of their crops with compost and others with chemical fertilizer. They found that the crops treated with compost gave yields that were as good or even better than those treated with chemical fertilizer. Once the quality of the land improved, farmers were able to plant a variety of additional crops, such as tomatoes and chili peppers, thereby improving their diet and nutrition. A well-balanced diet is important in reducing poverty because poor diet can affect health and undermine the ability of people to work and earn a living.

WHAT WOULD YOU DO?

You Are in Charge
You are a villager in Mozambique, and you have had to deal with drought, flood damage, and war. How best can you work with other villagers to maintain community life and improve food security?

- Since people have little money, return to non-cash bartering (exchange) among the villagers for goods and services.
- Diversify farming and grow different kinds of crops.
- Form a farming association and try out new farming methods.

CHAPTER 5

Global Trade

Ghana's economy in 2015 is in a desperate condition. This African country relies on the export of cocoa and gold. The world price of cocoa has been falling since World War II, and modest price increases over the past ten years have not reversed the general decline. Since the World Free Trade Agreement of 2011, no country has been permitted either to tax imports or to control imports of agricultural products from other countries. As a result, local farmers can no longer compete with cheap food imports. As Maryama from Zugu village, northern Ghana, says: "We used to rely on income from rice and corn farming, but we had to give up farming altogether because we could no longer make a living from it. Life is more difficult than it was for my parents' generation. My children's bellies are swollen with hunger."

The Terms of Trade

Global trading has brought benefits to people all over the world and access to many low-priced goods. However, developing countries have experienced problems because of the terms of trade—the price at which a country can sell its exports compared to what it has to pay for its imports. When the terms are unfair, poor farmers and factory workers do not earn enough from selling their products and services, and they remain stuck in poverty. Large international organizations play a dominant role in forming trade policies, especially the World Trade Organization (WTO), which had 149 member countries in 2005. Officially, all the members contribute to decision making. In practice, however, negotiations often take place among small groups of countries, and the developing countries are frequently excluded.

Trade Liberalization

Most sub-Saharan African countries depend on exporting agricultural goods, such as cocoa, sugar, and tea. In the 1970s, the terms set on trade went against the producers of these goods. They received lower prices for their products but had to pay higher prices for imports (especially oil,

These workers in Naivasha, Kenya, are preparing flowers for export. Flowers are a modern cash crop, grown in large quantities and exported thousands of miles (kilometers) away to be sold in Europe.

which hit record high prices during the 1970s). Many sub-Saharan countries experienced huge economic problems. During the 1980s, international banks imposed trade liberalization policies on most African economies and made developing countries open up their markets to allow other countries to sell them goods—even if they produced those goods themselves. The poor countries, however, are not allowed to support their agriculture and industry with subsidies, so their own products are more expensive than the imports. If the trade rules were fair, developed countries would have to allow unrestricted imports from developing countries as well. The governments in developed countries, however, subsidize their own farmers and industries and restrict imports from developing countries. The Organization for Economic Cooperation and Development (OECD) says that developed countries pay their farmers more than $300 billion per year in subsidies. World Bank surveys show that while almost half the people in the world live on less than $2 per day, a cow in Japan is suported by a subsidy of $7 a day, and a cow in the European Union by a subsidy of $2.20.

WHO'S WHO?: INTERNATIONAL ORGANIZATIONS

The World Trade Organization (WTO) negotiates trade agreements between countries.

The International Monetary Fund (IMF) supports international trade. If a country cannot pay for its imports, it can borrow money from the IMF and, in return, must follow economic policies laid down by the organization.

The World Bank lends money from developed countries to developing countries for projects (roads, dams, bridges, electricity) to help them develop and works to encourage trade to promote economic growth.

For example, in the United States, the government subsidizes rice farming to guarantee farmers a minimum income. The subsidy system means that farmers produce huge amounts of rice—more than is required by the home market. To get rid of the surplus, they sell it at low prices on the world market. This cost reduction has an effect on producers elsewhere. Rice growers in Artibonite Valley, Haiti, used to make a good living, but since a 1986 agreement, made at the request of the IMF and other lenders to Haiti, the government has had to permit cheap rice imports, mostly from the United States. Many farmers in Artibonite have now sold their land and moved to the city. Such policies have destroyed large sectors of agricultural production in developing countries.

NUMBER OF PEOPLE EMPLOYED IN EXPORT PROCESSING ZONES, 2000-2003

Region	Number in employment
North Africa	440,515
Sub-Saharan Africa	431,348
Middle East	691,397
Asia (including 30 million in China)	36,824,231
Mexico and Central America	2,241,821
South America and Caribbean	537,273
Europe	296,449
United States and Canada	330,000
Others	141,099
TOTAL	**41,934,133**

Source: International Labour Organization, 2003

Manufacturing

Some developing countries, such as South Korea, have made their economies less reliant on farming by building factories and exporting manufactured goods. In many cases, however, the terms of trade for manufactured goods also work in favor of developed countries. The prices of manufactured goods from developing countries have fallen consistently since the end of the 1980s—and the prices of Chinese goods have dropped the furthest. That is why so many manufactured goods, including clothes, electronic equipment, and toys, come from China.

In many countries all over the world, but mostly in developing countries, transnational companies have established factories in Export Processing Zones (EPZs). Governments established these zones to attract transnational companies by offering tax incentives, such as not requiring import or export duties on products made there. Foreign investors often pay no income tax or property tax for several years.

In developing countries, Export Processing Zones help relieve poverty to some extent because they create jobs. Their impact is limited, however, because foreign companies take so much of the profit away. Wages are usually very low, limiting the local people's ability to spend money on goods and services. Many workers live in poverty in spite of working long hours, and job conditions are often harsh. The Canadian journalist Naomi Klein has written about the Cavite EPZ in the Philippines, where the regular work shift is from 7 a.m. to 10 p.m. and employees sometimes have to work until 2 a.m. Those who refuse to work overtime may lose their jobs. One worker, Carmelita Alonzo, pleaded with her boss for time off because she was suffering from pneumonia. Her boss refused her the time, and she subsequently died of exhaustion due to overwork. Employees have no contracts and no paid leave. Their poverty makes them vulnerable, and workers know someone is always waiting to take their places if they cause trouble.

Workers in developed countries are also affected by the establishment of EPZs. Many international companies have closed factories in the United States and in Europe to move operations to countries such as China and India where labor is cheaper. In many cases, unemployment and poverty follows the loss of thousands of manufacturing jobs.

At this factory in Zhangmutou, China, workers make toys for international companies, including U.S. superstore Walmart. The toys are cheap mainly because the workers who make them are paid very low wages.

Fair Trade

Since the 1980s, a movement known as Fair Trade has worked to help farmers and workers in developing countries. Under a typical Fair Trade agreement, producers receive a minimum guaranteed price for goods such as coffee, tea, or cocoa. The price is higher than the normal market price and stays the same for a long time, giving farmers some security and allowing them to plan for the future. The agreement also lays down minimum standards to make sure workers are treated well and farmers protect the environment.

In Ghana, most farmers receive a low price for the cocoa they sell to European countries to be made into chocolate. In 1993, some cocoa farmers in the Kumasi region set up a cooperative, Kuapa

Fair Trade coffee on sale at a British supermarket. In Britain, 20 percent of the ground coffee sold in supermarkets in 2005 was fairly traded.

THE GROWTH OF FAIR TRADE

- U.S. imports of Fair Trade certified coffee grew about 75 percent per year between 1998 and 2004, and were worth $370 million in 2004.
- In twenty-five European countries, the net retail value of Fair Trade products grew about 20 percent per year between 2000 and 2005 and was worth more than $811 million in 2005.

Kokoo (Good Cocoa Farmers' Company). The cooperative pays the farmers a fair price for their beans. It sells cocoa to Fair Trade organizations in developed countries and uses some of the proceeds for community projects, such as building new wells. In 1998, Kuapa Kokoo was one of the founding members of The Day Chocolate Company, which produces Divine brand chocolate. Using beans from Kuapa Kokoo, the Divine brand is manufactured in Europe and marketed directly to supermarkets and on the Internet in Europe, Canada, and the United States.

Fair Rules

A change in international trade rules could make a big difference to many producers in developing countries. Organizations such as Oxfam say that agricultural producers should be paid more money for their products and that developed countries should not be allowed to sell subsidized farm products in developing countries. According to Oxfam, when developing countries export to developed countries, they face tariffs that are four times higher than developed countries have to pay. If the tariffs were equal, developing countries could sell goods to developed countries more easily. Reformers also say that transnational companies should be properly regulated to make sure they offer good working conditions.

The power to achieve change lies with the WTO and the IMF. These organizations listen to national governments, especially those of the developed countries.

In recent years, some developing countries have formed alliances to increase their bargaining power. The G3, for example, consists of India, Brazil, and South Africa. At a WTO meeting in Hong Kong in 2005, the developing countries formed another loose alliance called the G110 that secured an international agreement to end export subsidies by 2013. The alliaince is a good start. If trade becomes fairer, poverty can be reduced in developing countries.

WHAT WOULD YOU DO?

You are in charge
You hold an important office at the World Trade Organization. You think that developing countries are not being treated fairly. You have begun talking to people about making changes.

List three common practices that you wish to change.

CHAPTER 6

The Burden of Debt

It is October 2015. Representatives of the G11 (the expanded G8, now including China, India, and Brazil) are meeting to discuss the debt of the poorest countries–including India itself–in light of their failure to meet the UN Millenium Development Goals. Today, they are discussing Zambia. In 2006, this southern African country benefited from cancellation of its foreign debt. Zambia still had other debts to pay, however, and had to borrow more money to finance economic growth. It slashed its health services to pay these debts. Life expectancy has plummeted from thirty-five in 2005 to an even more shocking thirty as AIDS continues to take its toll in Zambia.

Deep in Debt

Poor countries got into debt in the 1960s and 1970s when they borrowed money for development from international organizations such as the International Monetary Fund and World Bank. Interest rates were low, and, in some cases, corrupt leaders ran up huge debts and left them as an undeserved legacy for their people. For example, in 1980, Zaire—now the Democratic Republic of Congo—had $5 billion in debts. Much of the borrowed money, however, was stolen or squandered by President Mobutu Sese Seko during his time in office (1965–97). Mobutu amassed a fortune—probably billions of dollars—and when he finally fled the country in 1997, he left it with $12 billion in debts.

During the early 1980s interest rates increased, and many poor countries found they could not pay back their debts. This situation

Gold miners dig huge pits in the Democratic Republic of Congo. Competition over gold wealth has created conflict in the region, bringing misery rather than prosperity.

became known as the *debt crisis*. In response, the IMF devised programs to encourage the indebted countries to focus on exports so they could earn money to pay off their debts. The programs offered more loans on condition that the poor countries made drastic cuts in spending. As a result, governments often cut back public-service expenditures, such as health, education, and social services, to save money. The new loans were known as *conditionalities*—loans offered under certain conditions. Although the welfare cuts increased poverty and caused several social crises, the IMF's policies have continued in various ways.

How Serious Is the Debt Problem?

The countries with the heaviest debts spend so much in debt repayments that they cannot spend money on measures to reduce poverty. For example, for every U.S. dollar that Mali spends on health, it spends $1.60 repaying its debt. If the international finance organizations controlled by the developed countries would forgive debts, the governments of developing countries could increase spending on crucial services such as health and education that can help to reduce poverty.

THE HEAVILY INDEBTED POOR COUNTRIES

The Heavily Indebted Poor Countries (HIPC) have the highest levels of poverty in the world and the least ability to pay off their debts. On the average, their debts are more than four times their annual earnings from exports and 120 percent of their Gross National Income (GNI). There are forty countries in this situation, most of them in sub-Saharan Africa.

- **Africa:** Benin, Burkina Faso, Burundi, Cameroon, Central African Republic, Chad, Comoros, Côte d'Ivoire, Democratic Republic of Congo, Eritrea, Ethiopia, Gambia, Ghana, Guinea, Guinea-Bissau, Guyana, Liberia, Madagascar, Malawi, Mali, Mauritania, Mozambique, Niger, Rwanda, São Tomé Príncipe, Senegal, Sierra Leone, Somalia, Sudan, Tanzania, Togo, Uganda, Zambia
- **Central and South America:** Bolivia, Haiti, Honduras, Nicaragua
- **Asia:** Kyrgyzstan, Nepal

Debt Relief

The Heavily Indebted Poor Countries (HIPC) Initiative of 1996 was designed to cut the debt of the poorest countries to a level that they could afford to pay. The developed countries, however, calculated the payments based on how much they believed the HIPC countries could pay rather than on how much debt relief the countries actually needed to relieve poverty. Progress was slow, and few countries benefited. By 2005, barely 10 percent of the total debt owed by HIPC countries had been canceled.

In 2005, the G8 agreed to forgive large parts of the debts owed by one-third of the poorest countries to the African Development Fund, the International Development Association, and the IMF as long as these countries met IMF and World Bank requirements. This action was called the Multilateral Debt Relief Initiative. In July 2006, seventeen HIPC countries began to receive this debt relief.

Zambia is one of the countries that qualifies for debt relief. In the early 2000s, the government privatized public utilities, allowed foreign imports, and removed subsidies for its exports. Finance Minister Ngandu Maganda said in early 2006 that Zambia's total foreign debt would be reduced from $7 billion to $500 million by the end of the year. In April 2006, the government announced it would use some of the money freed by debt relief to pay for health care in rural areas. It is still committed to the tight control of public spending expected under the HIPC initiative, so paying for additional health-care workers and medicines will be difficult. The finance minister has warned that it will take a generation to see the benefits of poverty-cutting measures.

Reducing the debt of the poorest countries has seen some progress. HIPC countries may, however, find they have to hold down

LIMITATIONS OF DEBT RELIEF

In 2004, one of the world's poorest countries, Niger in western Africa, received debt relief under HIPC. According to an international aid organization, 40 percent of the money saved by debt cancellation is going to education. Nevertheless, Niger still has no hope of achieving the development goal for education. In 2002, world leaders established the Education Fast Track Initiative to tackle this problem, and donations from developed countries were meant to finance nearly nine thousand classrooms and recruit nine thousand teachers in Niger. Few donors paid up, however. Nearly two hundred thousand children who would have received an education under the plan could not go to school. The poorest countries clearly need more than debt relief to solve their problems.

public spending or acquire further debts. If the international community changed unfair trade rules, commodity prices would change, and then the poorest countries might be able to progress with debt reduction.

WHAT WOULD YOU DO?

You Are in Charge
You are a leading member of a campaign to drop the debt. What will you call for?

1. Cancellation of all unpayable debts of poor countries with no economic conditions attached.
2. Cancellation of all unpayable debts as long as poor countries follow IMF conditions.
3. Reduction of debts to levels that poor countries can afford.

An Indonesian student wearing a mask holds up a banner during a protest in Jakarta, Indonesia, against the G8 summit held in Scotland in 2005. Many reformers called for the immediate cancellation of the debts of the poorest countries.

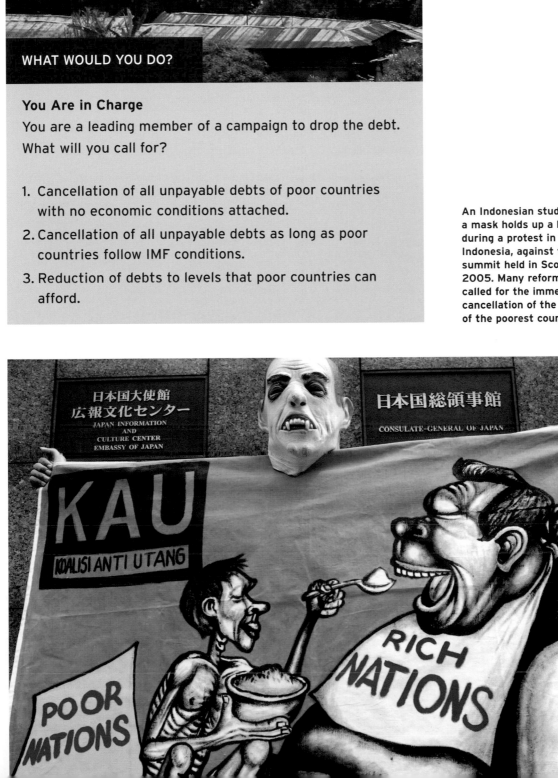

CHAPTER 7

Aid and Development

Zoya, from Muzaffarabad in Pakistan, was three years old when she survived the tremendous earthquake that hit the north of her country in 2005. Her family was unable to return to their devastated city. They received emergency aid at first and temporary shelter. Over the next few years, however, the world was hit by increasingly violent earthquakes and hurricanes. The $6.2 billion in aid and loans pledged by donor countries to rebuild the ravaged communities in Pakistan never arrived. Ten years later, Zoya's family remains in its makeshift home. Her parents have no regular work because economic reconstruction in the earthquake region never occurred. Zoya says, "Emergency aid saved our lives, and we are very grateful, but once the emergency was over, we were forgotten."

Not Enough

Aid can be invaluable. It can provide people with desperately needed assistance during emergencies and help rebuild their communities afterward. Aid can help poor countries finance health, education, and other vital services. Yet there are problems with aid. First, it is insufficient. Most rich countries have not increased their aid to 0.7 percent of their national incomes as they promised to do in the 1970s. In 2005, the G8 pledged to increase aid by $48 billion each year until 2010. This aid boost is urgently needed. Although aid money appears to flow from rich to poor countries, far more money flows in the opposite direction. For every $2 they receive in aid, poor countries spend $6 in debt repayments.

The Indian Red Cross brings medicines to help survivors of the Pakistan earthquake of 2005. The earthquake left three hundred thousand people homeless. Within a few months, most returned home, but tens of thousands remained in temporary camps.

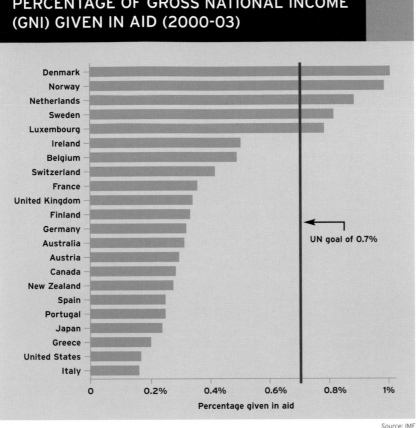

PERCENTAGE OF GROSS NATIONAL INCOME (GNI) GIVEN IN AID (2000-03)

Denmark
Norway
Netherlands
Sweden
Luxembourg
Ireland
Belgium
Switzerland
France
United Kingdom
Finland
Germany
Australia
Austria
Canada
New Zealand
Spain
Portugal
Japan
Greece
United States
Italy

UN goal of 0.7%

0   0.2%   0.4%   0.6%   0.8%   1%

Percentage given in aid

Source: IMF

Of the countries shown on this graph, only Denmark, Norway, the Netherlands, Sweden, and Luxembourg have met the UN target to provide 0.7 percent of their gross national income in aid.

Inappropriate?

In some cases, aid pays for costly projects, such as dam building, that promote a country's development but do not necessarily benefit the poorest people. Much debate goes on over whether to give aid for such projects. Dams are built for many reasons: to control flooding, to produce water power to provide electricity, and to provide water for irrigation. Dams can be engines of economic development that can modernize a region the same way that new airports and highways can. For example, the Bakun Dam in Malaysia is a symbol of the country's progress toward becoming an advanced modern economy. Building a dam, however, alters the flow of a river, floods its valley, and usually has wide-ranging environmental impact. In many cases, thousands of people have to move from an area because the dam will create a flood behind it, and people lose their homes and livelihoods, often without receiving adequate compensation in return.

Tied Aid

Aid is often offered only if certain conditions are met. For example, to qualify for 92 percent of Italy's aid funds, countries receiving that aid are required to purchase goods and services from Italian companies. The money is not spent in the most appropriate way for the local people. The conditions can even make poverty worse. In the 1990s, as a condition for giving aid and debt relief, the World Bank and Britain encouraged Tanzania to privatize the water supply system in its capital, Dar es Salaam. As part of the plan, Britain gave $17.5 million in aid to Tanzania between 1998 and 2004 to promote privatization. After privatization was completed in 2002, however, the service grew worse. The Tanzanian government claimed that City Water, a British-German-Tanzanian company that took charge of Dar es Salaam's water supply, did not keep its promises and failed to contribute to a fund to pay for water supplies for the very poor. Customers complained that the water service was irregular and that when water did not come through, they had to buy supplies from street vendors. The company claimed it was losing money and raised its prices. In May 2005, angry customers forced the government to end its contract with City Water.

Corruption

Corruption in public office—government workers taking bribes for their own benefit—is a worldwide problem. Some critics of aid argue that giving aid to the poorest countries is pointless because corrupt officials simply steal the money. Corruption is, in fact, most obvious in some of the least developed countries. The World Bank has tracked public spending to estimate how much of aid money spent on health and education disappears and fails to reach its destination. A survey of 155 facilities in Uganda in 2000 found that 70 percent of specific drugs and supplies had disappeared. Fighting corruption is important to help ensure that the poorest people benefit from aid. Some experts argue that not giving aid to a developing

In Sierra Leone, people rely on a public faucet in the street for their water. The World Health Organization estimates that only 28 percent of the population have access to clean water. The state-run water company is in crisis. Britain has encouraged the government to privatize the water supply, but evidence from countries such as Tanzania indicates that this policy is unlikely to improve service.

country because it is seen as corrupt can mean deeper poverty for its inhabitants. Others contend that if a high level of corruption exists, the aid is unlikely to benefit the poorest citizens so it is better to withdraw aid altogether.

Effective Aid

How can aid be more effective? First, the amount of aid could be increased, as the G8 promised to do. New options for raising extra money by other means than taxing individuals could help the international community achieve its target. Economists and some nonprofit aid organizations have proposed global taxes, for example, on airline tickets and foreign exchange transactions. Second, it is important to make sure aid is directed toward health, education, and basic services. Many development experts also argue that it would be better if aid donations were not conditional on the country carrying out particular economic reforms, such as the privatization of services.

This graph shows how much of the total aid for social services in developing countries comes from specific developed countries. These services include public hospitals and clinics, roads, clean water, electricity, garbage collection, and telecommunications, all of which improve people's standards of living.

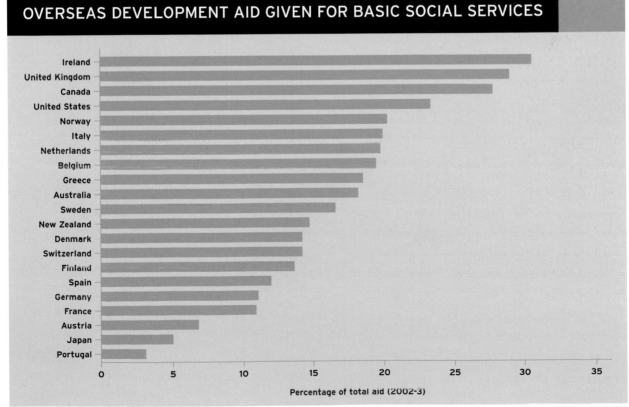

OVERSEAS DEVELOPMENT AID GIVEN FOR BASIC SOCIAL SERVICES

Percentage of total aid (2002-3)

Source: Human Development Report 2005

Development

Instead of depending on aid, developing countries would do better to focus on development. They cannot develop in the same way that already developed nations did, however. Several European countries built their industries using wealth from other countries they had conquered. They introduced import controls such as tariffs to protect their growing industries from competition. Working people campaigned for better living and working conditions, so governments brought in social service measures. Today, developing countries are expected to advance without these forms of protection. If they succeed, they will be able to produce low-cost goods for a huge, worldwide market and still pay local people a decent wage.

Economic development, however, does not necessarily lead to a reduction in poverty. As Joseph Stiglitz, former chief economist at the World Bank said: "In Latin America, growth has not been accompanied by a reduction in inequality or even a reduction in poverty. In some cases, poverty has actually increased, as evidenced by the urban slums that dot the landscape. . . . Clearly, growth alone does not always improve the lives of all a country's people."

How Should Developing Countries Move Forward?

Experts do not agree about the path developing countries should take to develop and reduce poverty. People who favor globalization, such as the leaders of the World Bank, believe that the answer lies in involving developing countries in more international business. So far, Asia has gained a great deal from globalization, but Latin America and the Caribbean have not. Globalization has actually hurt sub-Saharan Africa and central Asia. The supporters of globalization say this is because all people are not participating in the global economy yet. Many antipoverty campaigners argue that globalization has increased inequality. They

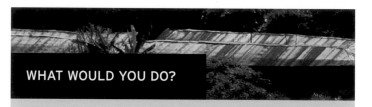

WHAT WOULD YOU DO?

You are in charge
You are a U.S. senator who wants the United States to increase its international aid from 0.18 percent to 0.7 percent of its gross national income. Which one of the following strategies would you recommend to obtain the money?

■　Increase taxation on the wealthiest.

■　Deduct the money from U.S military spending.

■　Set up a lottery to raise money for aid.

believe that each country should figure out for itself the best way to get involved in the global economy rather than following the recommendations of the World Bank and the IMF.

In some cases, developing countries have made economic agreements to help one another without relying on the World Bank and the IMF. For example, in 2005, Venezuela and Cuba agreed to share technological developments. Venezuela promised to pay salaries to fifteen thousand Cuban medical professionals to train Venezuelan doctors and health-care specialists. In return, Venezuela promised to set a maximum price for the oil they sold to Cuba at $27 a barrel instead of the market price of $44 a barrel.

This fifty-eight-year-old Venezuelan man is learning to read and write through a literacy program in Caracas, Venezuela. Improving literacy rates plays an important part in a country's development.

CHAPTER 8

What If We Act Now?

It is 2015. International finance organizations, transnational companies, governments, and nonprofit aid organizations have made a big effort to work together. All the rich countries now provide 0.7 percent of their national income in aid. They have contributed another $94 billion a year so that all the UN Millenium Development Goals could be met. Virtually the entire global population has access to clean water and sanitation, most malaria sufferers receive a cure, and the majority of people with HIV/AIDS have access to drugs to help them to stay healthy and prolong their lives. Nearly all the children in the world complete primary education.

What Can Governments Do?

If governments lived up to the promises they made when they formed the UN Millenium Development Goals, absolute poverty could be halved by 2015. In fact, absolute poverty could be eliminated altogether if world leaders made a small change in their spending priorities. Just 1 percent of the national income of every country on the globe ($403 billion in 2004) would be enough to achieve this goal. This figure sounds like a lot of money. Compared to world military expenditure, however—estimated at $1,035 billion in 2004—it is very little. The United States alone is responsible for half this military spending.

Within all countries, both rich and poor, governments could reduce inequalities among their own citizens and decrease the number of people living in poverty. They could raise taxes for the very wealthy, for example, and spend the money to improve the conditions of the poorest in their societies. Some people believe such policies may also promote economic growth. Others believe that high taxation for top earners could remove the incentive to develop businesses and create wealth, and could, therefore, slow down growth.

INTERNATIONAL CAMPAIGN TO END POVERTY

The Global Call to Action Against Poverty was launched in 2005 to put pressure on national governments to meet their commitments to the MDGs. It is now the largest-ever anti-poverty alliance. Its organizations represent more than 150 million people globally, and it is active in more than eighty countries.

Government action can plant the seeds of change. In Latin American countries such as Chile, Bolivia, and Venezuela, governments are attempting to improve the lives of the poorest in society. In Venezuela, the government has set up *missiones*—special projects to deliver health, education, and housing services. More than 1 million of the poorest children now receive a free education, and 1.2 million illiterate adults have learned to read and write. Ordinary people have set up worker cooperatives where everyone receives the same wage and takes part in decision making.

Bolivia is one of Latin America's poorest nations even though it has the region's second largest natural gas reserves after Venezuela. President Evo Morales, elected in 2005, claimed that foreign companies received too much profit from Bolivia's gas industry. In 2006, his government nationalized the country's natural gas and oil sectors so that the profits could be used for the benefit of the Bolivian people.

Indigenous Bolivians march in May 2005 to put pressure on the government of President Carlos Mesa to nationalize the country's natural gas resources. The president resigned over the issue the following month, and Evo Morales was elected in December.

Grassroots Movements

Regardless of their governments, poor communities around the world have shown that they can take action to improve their own situations. In Brazil, less than 3 percent of the population owns two-thirds of the land. Half the land lies idle, while 4 million farmers are landless and homeless. A powerful grassroots movement, the Landless Workers' Movement, organizes landless farmers to take over unoccupied land and establish cooperative farms. Since 1985, it has won land titles (the legal right to own the land) for more than 350,000 landless families. As of 2006, approximately 180,000 families were waiting for the government to recognize their right to land occupied by the movement. The movement has built houses, schools, and clinics. It has organized a distribution system that makes sure that farm products are sold at prices that are fair to the producers. With land, food pricing security, and fairer trading arrangements, the farmers have emerged from poverty.

The Grameen Bank has helped this Bangladeshi woman to set up a business and lift herself out of poverty. She owns a small transportation agency and a minibus that she bought using a loan from the bank.

44

Microcredit

Another example comes from Bangladesh. In 1976, the Grameen Bank of Bangladesh started offering microcredit—small loans to landless rural laborers who had never been able to borrow money before. By July 2004, the bank had 3.7 million borrowers, 90 percent of them women. The women have used the loans to set up small businesses, such as pottery making, weaving, and sewing. They have improved their homes and their children's diet. This success story proves that extending a small amount of credit to the poorest people in society can enable them to find reasonably paid occupations and also repay their loans. The number of Grameen Bank members living below the poverty line in Bangladesh is 20 percent, compared to 50 percent of nonmembers. In 1997, the Grameen Bank model was adopted by the Grameen Foundation in the United States. By 2006, the foundation was working with microcredit institutions in twenty-two countries.

What Can We Do?

You can do plenty about poverty at home and abroad. You could campaign for your government to take action on poverty by writing letters to your representatives. You could give some time to support a charity that works to reduce poverty, such as organizations that help local homeless people or refugees, for example. At school you could raise awareness by setting up a discussion group or organizing a fundraising event. When you shop, try to buy fair trade goods.

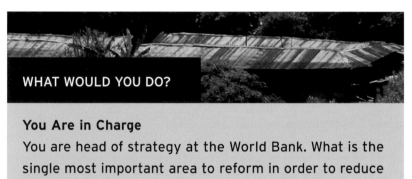

WHAT WOULD YOU DO?

You Are in Charge
You are head of strategy at the World Bank. What is the single most important area to reform in order to reduce world poverty?

- ■ Reduce poor countries' foreign debt.
- ■ Make trade rules fairer to poor countries.
- ■ Increase aid payments.

Everyone needs to act, both rich and poor. The majority of the world's people merely want enough to eat, decent health and educational services, and some security. The resources are available to provide these simple needs. If the countries of the world worked together, we could end absolute poverty by 2015.

Glossary

absolute poverty A person living in absolute poverty, as defined by the United Nations, survives on just $1 a day; many people in absolute poverty lack basic food, clothing, and shelter

antiretroviral therapy (ART) Treatment with drugs that help stop the HIV virus from multiplying in the body

cash crop A crop that is produced for sale

colony A land that is ruled by people from another country

conditionalities Certain conditions applied to a loan that a country must fulfill to borrow the money

cooperative A business owned and run by its members, who share the profits

dalit A member of the lowest caste, or class, in Indian society; dalits used to be known as *untouchables* because they carried out the dirtiest jobs in society

debt relief An arrangement by which a country is allowd not to pay some of its debt to reduce the burden of debt repayments

developed countries Also known as the First World or the countries of the North; they include all the regions of Europe plus northern America, Australia, New Zealand, and Japan

developing countries Also known as the Third World or the countries of the South; developing countries include all the regions of Africa, Asia (except for Japan), Latin America, and the Caribbean, plus Melanesia, Micronesia and Polynesia.

duties (export/import) Taxes paid on items exported to another country or imported into a country

Fair Trade A system in which companies deal directly with producers and fix a fair price for their goods over a period of time; the goods are produced in a way that ensures that producers work in safe conditions and look after the environment

G8 An organization made up of the richest countries in the world: the United States, France, the Russian Federation, Great Britain, Germany, Japan, Italy, and Canada

globalization A process through which countries around the world have become increasingly linked to each other through the rapid growth of trade, communications, travel, and culture

Gross National Income (GNI) The total value of goods and services produced within a country, plus its income received from other countries (such as interest payments on loans), minus similar payments made to other countries

hygiene The practice of keeping clean to prevent disease

indigenous people The people who originally lived in a country before it was settled by other peoples

literacy rate The number of adults in the country who can read

malnourished The resulting poor condition of health caused by a lack of food or a lack of healthy food

Millennium Development Goals (MDGs) Eight key goals adopted by the United Nations in 2000 that include ending extreme poverty and hunger, improving health, achieving primary education for all children, promoting equality between the sexes, and protecting the environment; all the UN member states agreed to try to achieve the goals by 2015

nonprofit aid organization A charity or other association that is independent of government or business

poverty line A level of annual income below which a household is defined to be living in poverty; the poverty line varies from country to country

primary health care Health care provided by a doctor or nurse, with whom the patient first has contact; if necessary, the patient is referred to a specialist

privatize To turn a publicly owned or controlled business, industry, or service into a privately controlled one

relative poverty People in relative poverty are poor in relation to the vast majority of other people in their society; if most people in a society have access to goods such as a car and a telephone and someone cannot afford these items, then that person is in relative poverty

sanitation The equipment and systems that keep places clean, especially the provision of clean water and the disposal of sewage—human waste

slum An area of a city that is very poor and where the houses are in bad condition

sub-Saharan Africa The region of Africa that lies south of the Sahara; it includes the countries of east, central, west and southern Africa

subsidy Money that is paid, often by a government, to reduce the costs of producing goods or services so that their prices can be kept low

subsistence farming Farming that provides the basic needs of farmers and their families with little or no surplus to sell on the market

sustainability Using resources so that they are not damaged or completely depleted

tariff A tax that is paid on goods coming into or going out of a country

transnational company A company that operates in several different countries, especially a large and powerful company

United Nations (UN) An association of 191 states (2005), including almost all of the internationally recognized independent nations of the world, that works to improve economic and social conditions and to solve political problems in a peaceful way

World Health Organization (WHO) An agency of the United Nations that coordinates international efforts to fight disease and promote health

Further Information

Books

Bowden, Rob. *World Poverty*. Face the Facts (series). Heinemann, 2003).

Jarman, Melanie. *Rich World, Poor World*. What's Your View? (series). Franklin Watts, 2006

Maddocks, Steven. *World Hunger*. Twenty-first Century Issues (series). World Almanac, 2004

Stearman, Kaye. *Poverty* World Issues (series). Chrysalis Children's Books, 2005.

Web Sites

The Fairtrade Foundation
www.fairtrade.org.uk
Information about Fair Trade products and how Fair Trade works.

Jubilee USA Network
www.jubileeusa.org
An American organization that campaigns to cancel the debts of the poorest countries to help them fight poverty.

Oxfam International
www.oxfam.org/en
Oxfam is a development and campaign organization that works in more than one hundred countries to find lasting solutions to poverty.

Save the Children
www.savethechildren.org
The website of the charity Save the Children that helps children worldwide who suffer from poverty. .

The World Bank
www.worldbank.org/
The site has details of development projects worldwide with statistical information about all countries.

Publisher's note to educators and parents: Our editors have carefully reviewed these Web sites to ensure that they are suitable for children. Many Web sites change frequently, however, and we cannot guarantee that a site's future contents will continue to meet our high standards of quality and educational value. Be advised that children should be closely supervised whenever they access the Internet.

What Would You Do?

p. 7
Eradicating extreme poverty and hunger and providing education about HIV/AIDS might be your two top goals.
You might offer free advice and training in specific industries to help the Zambians help themselves.
You might try to raise money in Britain for a Zambian public-health education fund, explaining that Britain has a moral debt to Zambia.

Page 13:
All of these areas are important, but HIV/AIDS has had such a catastrophic effect on the continent that halting its spread must be a priority.

Page 19:
1. Many parents cannot afford to pay tuition or other school fees.
2. Children are needed to work in the fields.
3. The schools have very little equipment.
4. The government puts all its money into repaying national debt.

Several school costs may not be necessary, including uniforms and sports equipment. Do not require these, and costs will be less.

Page 25:
This story is a real-life example from Nwadjahane in southern Mozambique, and, in fact, all three changes were made.
1. Returning to non-cash bartering allows villagers with little money to exchange labor with others in a similar position. The exchange leads to increased solidarity between the villagers.
2. Diversifying into growing different kinds of crops spreads risk.
3. If people work in a group, they can share the risk of trying new ideas. If a new practice is unsuccessful for some farmers, others can help them out, while successful methods can be passed on.

Page 31:
1. Unfair trade rules let developed countries subsidize their farmers and charge less for their products than farmers in developing countries.
2. Developing countries must pay high tariffs on imports.
3. Manufacturers in EPZS pay their workers very poorly.

Page 35:
Because of the failure to achieve significant debt relief, the international Drop the Debt campaign calls for the cancellation of all the unpayable debts of poor countries without conditions so that these countries can spend the money saved on development.

Page 40:
You could argue that generous international aid would buy sufficient good-will to eliminate the need for its equivalent in military spending.

Page 45:
Reducing foreign debt will be helpful, enabling developing countries to spend money on useful services. Making trade rules fairer is crucial; if developing countries received a fair price for their exports, their economic situation could improve. An increase in aid payments can be helpful if it is not tied aid but will have little benefit without debt reduction and a change in trade rules.

Index